Deadly Ending Season

Deadly Ending Season

DESMOND JOHNSON

AKIRA PRESS

First published in Great Britain 1984
by Akira Press
PO BOX 409
London E2 7EU
printed in Great Britain by
Redwood Burn Limited
Trowbridge, Wiltshire

British Library Cataloguing in Publication Data

Johnson, Desmond
Deadly ending season.
I Title
811 PR9265.9.J6/

ISBN 0-947638-00-8
ISBN 0-947638-01-6 Pbk

for ERICA

CONTENTS

DEADLY
ENDING
SEASON

YARD TALK
no-no
      b
        r
          o
            k
              e
                n
inglish
mi a knuckle up buckle up an chuckle up
mi words
like the stammer of sentences in de bottom
of some people's throat
yard talk inglish into submission
till mi pat-wa bus tru an conquer
full a history an roots
full a love and creation
fa yard talk a compulsory
fa I an I an I an I
NOW an in de nex IWA
fa like mi fada an mi mada
de chip never fly far from de block.

MASS JOBE

And so
we all gone old in inglan
mi an sister lizza
brada ferd
an sister matty
an inglish man
an inglish woman
with a yard
with a yard
with a yard indentity
our memories of the past
are so plenty
how we first come here
in winter time
got a bustraining
to earn little dime
did train shunting
and office cleaning
did road sweeping
and can-packaging
did bread baking
and house building
did hospital work
on various wings
were aux-
iliary
nurse
and kitchen porter
guardman
teawoman
and cleaner
am speaking
from a standpoint of age
'perience
my sons and daughters
experience!

11

we were railman
railwoman
train drivers
signal man
and controller
collectors of tickets
and night workers
our best years spent
on british rail
our years went by
like a fairy tale
am speaking
from a standpoint of age
'perience
my sons and daughters
experience!
we sen back money
to o' people a yard
say life is good
it was tough and hard
and we have children
plus those back a yard
we have children
o lord! lord! lord!
and to make enns meet
we work seven days a week
on sundays as well
'till we body get weak
at nights as well
'till we run right down
with physical ailments
and nerves breakdown
am speaking
from a standpoint of age
'perience
my sons and daughters experience!

the beauty that we had
the strength that we had
was reduce and reduce
dear lord my God!
like wasted life
and wasted time
we have nothing to show
not a penny
not a dime
only fruits of our body
our blood children
who are thrown like dogs
in a lion's den
I am looking
from a standpoint of age
'perience
at my sons and daughters
experience
in
Bristol
Brixton
Moss Side
and Merseyside
bawling to miself
there is little difference
still a wasted life
wasted time
without a job
without a dime
fuming
and raging
against this crime
it's from a standpoint of age
and experience
that I know they shall win
and overcome

but for us it's late
to say 'if we know'
much too late to make a show
jus thank massa God
that mi live so long
to have a walk with the wife
still feeling strong
holding the wife
by a bus stop stand
going to friends
in the heart of Brixton
Railton Road
our new Kingston.

OLE CHARLIE BOY

Ole charlie boy
you still deh a inglan
charlie boy
you still deh a london
yes
   mi sey
      mi sey
         mi sey
            mi sey
yes
   mi sey
      mi sey
         mi sey
            mi sey
razing mi voice a likkle
e did fass
fe ask mi dat question
cause we both is in
de same position
for we both come
here in de fifties
a kinda runaway
from yard perplexities
an we all come find
de same sin-ting
low paid jobs
bad housing
so yes
   mi sey
      mi sey
         mi sey
            mi sey

yes
   mi sey
     mi sey
       mi sey
        mi sey
mi still on de dole
still in de hole
still is as bruck
and can't find no wok
what about your children
charlie boy
what about you plan dem
charlie boy
well
   mi sey
     mi sey
       mi sey
        mi sey
well
   mi sey
     mi sey
       mi sey
        mi sey
mi only boy is as worser than mi
dem sen him to prison
on dem new sus law
dem sen him to prison
cause dem catch him with a draw
and de gals dem a breeding agen
dem total children come to ten
de mada an mi is not so sweet
she sey all mi do is to walk de street

ole johnny boy
   time is rough
      ole johnny boy
         time is tough
mi save up so money
mi waa fe go home
telephone de airport people dem
ole johnny boy
   time is rough
      ole johnny boy
         time is tough
de cost fe de flight
is more dan wha mi have
coulda sell de house
if belong to mi
ole johnny boy
   time is rough
      ole johnny boy
         time is tough
mi ago die in inglan
johnny boy
we ago die in inglan
johnny boy
cause mi bruck in inglan
johnny boy
cause we bruck in inglan
johnny boy
ole johnny boy
   time is rough
      ole johnny boy
         time is tough!

BLACK MAJORITY

Graveyard Urbanity!
Deathtrap Psychology!
enforced
and re-enforced on we
Governments strategic weapons
creating Black Ghettos
Inner City Slums
and unemployment
to use the now
overused labels on us/on we
'Black Ethnic Minority?'
for the world to see
our tragedy
starving begging faces
bawling for help on
television screens
in Europe and The Americas
in the land of our
past and present oppressors
with hyporcrite presidents
and prime ministers
abusing power
in disguise
'oh we care for the Blacks'
they say
but a wen since
we tun minority
sons and daughters
of Afrikan decent
a wen
a wen since we are not majority
Afrikans uprooted
from homeland
that now we
are Blacks
instead of Afrikans

mi sey
a wen since we tun minority
living in concrete shacks
in rundown areas
a wen since we become
the victims of perpetual sabotage
living a no good life
in our urban
inner city ghettos
a wen since the Afrikans
abroad change race
that we can now
be called
Black Ethnic Minority
in dreadful poverty
inhumanity
in Britain
in rundown Britain
in America
in money bloated America
in the Caribbean
in the tourist resort Caribbean
a wen since we tun minority
dis new phrasing
Black Ethnic Minority
a wen! a wen!
it must be a plan
well planned
to pump fear in us
that if they gang
up on us
we must run in a hole
and bawl
'outnumber! outnumber!
surrender! surrender!
in hopelessness and despair
in fear fear fear

but we are not deceived
not! deceived
'bout dem minority
'bout dem minority
when it's
a Black Afrikan
Majority
chanting
and fighting
to be free.

DEADLY

you waa fe call mi dutty names
den gwaan noh!
you waa fe call mi low down
den gwaan noh!
you waa fe shout shout shout
shout abuses!
you waa fe curse curse curse
curse mi colour!
you waa fe shout shout shout
shout white power!
with you little dutty words
and slogans!
with words
on the walls
about
the 'Immigrants!'
you inhumane
little pagans!
gwaan! with your shouting
and cursing
for you silly
little words
can't move mi
your dirty
little words
can't bruise mi
or your
well
SIGN POSTED HATE RAGE
your
POL-
ICE
FORCE

or
prison cage
so call you dutty names
but noh touch mi
fa mi a come from a line
of Afrikans
born right here
in inglan
with the heart
and the strength
to fight the pagans
for if a death a death a death a
we we fight you
for if a death a death a death a
we we slay you
for if a death a death a death a
we we claat you
so gwaan!
   gwaan!
with you cave rage
   gwaan!
   gwaan!
with you hate rage
for it seems like
you waa fe taste
mi black rage
mi outrage!

TIME IS SHORT

I
We all can see
their wrong doings
dutty dutty jobs
and bad housing
ra-
cism
and the brain-washing
some gone mental
some gone spiritual
all jus a suffer by
the co-
lo-
nial
all jus a suffer by
the old criminal
they oppress us
everywhere we try to live
swearing to God that it's not mischief
the News Media
jus label us
Daily
Nightly
it insult us
and the dutty court houses
are so unjust
with black youth
black youth
frame for sus
with black youth
black youth
gone
serve time
gone
serve time

it's Brutality!
Police Crime!
we want amnesty
urgently!
humane cops
assualting must stop!
we ago
fight fe we rights
fight fe we rights

For right through
his'
twist story
de slave masters have all glory
now we ago
fight fe we rights
fight fe we rights
for once upon a time
we bowed to the whip
once upon a time
on de evil slave ship
once upon a time
we were chained as slaves
once upon a time
it became our graves
this once upon a time
they brought again
once upon a time
with a mental chain
with a whole population
in poverty
with a whole population
begging mercy
I can't contain
can't maintain
can't tolerate this mass murder
dem time is short
time is short
we ago fight fe we rights
fight fe we rights

upon time we rage
upon time we war
arms ina arms?
we all ago fight
for time is short
time is short.

SHE WAS SILENT

She escaped from the plantations
after many years of enslavement
to the highlands
mountainous highlands
Darliston
Grotto
Where she lived the rest of her life
where mother saw her
the old black woman
our great grandmother?
one hundred and five years old
wearing still
her long belted gown
her green gown
her slavery gown
and that was in the 1930's
the old woman
wouldn't say a thing
never
ever
once
mentioned slavery
she had gown old with it
grown old with her thoughts
her experiences
shut up
silent
with history
our history
the wickedness done to us
now causing us to rage
rage against the past
the old woman
the sea
the enslavers
for locking away our history

causing us to cry
tears of blood
but through our weeping
we see
we understand
and we forgave her
we forgave the old woman
wrinkled in her poverty
in pain
with a century
of torturing
whip marks
crisscrossed on her back
face
hands
head
her
her body
her face
a crumbling
her spirit broken
her mind
her thoughts
her heart
her being
a burden
awaiting
awaiting death's deliverance
and so we forgave her
for if she should speak
utter
a word about slavery
she would weep
we would weep
for she would stutter
and she would stutter
'how they
how they

how they raped me
how they . . . .
how they . . . .
how they . . . . lord! lord! lord!
my God!'
and she would break down
she would die
for her memory
is like a plague
that hurts
pain
bites
her face
a record of one hundred years
of terror
torture
unspoken
inhumanity
her hands
looking removed from her body
hang down her side
lifeless
living witness
of how she was
stretched
wrecked
by whiteman's inhumanity
insanity
her legs wobbling
they carry her around on stretcher
too weak to stand up
walk
broken
living record
of the miles
she was forced to walk
the days

29

nights
working
standing
chained
detained
one hundred years
years!
her eyes pulled in
sick
diseased
blind
with the evil she had seen
endured
her whole body
reminds all of the
days
The Dark Days
when Euro-
peans
Ameri-
cans
and Arabs
used then raped us
used then beat us
used then kill us
for money
fun
brutality
insanity
for years!
years!
years!!

THE BIGGER EVER BLAME

Lets fling the blame
let's fling the blame
let's fling the
big
ever
blame
the slave trade dealers
the dirty white shame
on the Euro-
peans
on the Ameri-
cans
who murder us still
us Fronts and Klans
a repayment is well overdue
their own destruction!
even that will do
let's fling the blame
let's fling the blame
let's fling it East and South
on the Arabs as well
who invent the Route
where seas
black
blood
were spilled for fun
for gold trinkets
under eastern sun
using our people
as their own property
for life
for wife
the man and child
were used like dogs
when old they died

by an Arab knife
an Arab hand
for years and years
around the desert land
let's fling the blame
let's fling the blame
let's fling it Far and Wide
at factions of tribes
our own people
who were used and used
as a slave vehicle
a Euro-
pean plan
disgraceful White Con
selling false teeth
false clothes
false-everything
promise as well
black captives take wings
on the evil slave ship
where millions died
that until now
we mourn even cried
for those who resist
and jumped overboard
for those who were sick
and were thrown overboard
for the millions
who died
in Euro-
pean chain
who were murdered
slaughtered
in death
detained
for those that died
on Ameri-
cans shores

for we are the children
that they bore
for those that died on plantations
in the Caribbean
for generations
for all our people
who were murdered by these brutes
for all of them
we say
WE SHALL FIGHT!
so fling the blame
fling the blame
for awareness now
as a trade like that
we'll never! ever! allow
a fight to the finish
but no life as slave
a fight and fight
'till oppression is a grave.

MY PEOPLE

We are tented rented
Then sold out,
Made to fail to become
A dropout,

We protested
And are prevented,
To express our thoughts
And miseries.

We have exploded,
Eroded,
Like a flood in
Its strength.

Our tidal waves
Are making graves,
By the movements
Of the wind,

North!
We shall attack you!
We shall attack you!
South, East and West too.

For in this fight
We are right;
The earth was made
For all.

ENDING

I am bom-
barded
bom-
barded
with false preachers
bom-
barded
bom-
barded
with false teachers
bellowing the rights of the poor people
preaching for the cause of the oppress people
collecting funds and con-
tri-
bu-
tions
regular tides
large don-
a-
tions
to boast their savings and refugees plans
to boast their wealth in Barclays Banks
they own countries
big
man-
sions
ex-
pen-
sive
shares
acres of land
while the poor and oppress
sinks lower lower
down

in their hell
in their hell
their shanty towns
while they danced and rejoice
in their
hy-
poc-
ri-
sy
praying to God
to have pity
enslaving the people
in deep poverty
laughing at faces
that are beggin' mercy
with their brutal policy
of destruction
widespread genocide
an-
nih-
ila-
tion
forcing the means
of
in-
sur-
rec-
tion
with freedom fighters
in every nation
and in the south
they are guer-
rillas
in the north
terror-
ists

all with the policy of total blitz
with bullets for their words
and liberation
with bullets for their fight
'gainst oppression
setting in motion
what was said before
'Destruction of the wicked
The Dirty White Whore!'

what a mess
what a mess
they are living in
lovers of dogs
hate
human
beings
perverted sex-
u-
al-
i-
ty
bent inclination tradition
manifest itself in generations
nuclear guards
and the BOMB users
destructive force
and false teachers
what a wicked
what an aweful
what a lying nation
believers of God
worshipping Satan!

THE PUPPETS IN AFRICA

'I am the mouth of the people
speaking for their rights,'
you boast on the screen
last Sunday night
but your system is borrowed
your knowledge not yours
you were taught by those
who hate our-
col-
our
they-made-you-what-you-are-
and-give-you-
pow-
er
so you like Great Britain
you like America
you like Europe
and you like Russia
you preach on sundays or
praise Allah in the Mosque
you speak Cambridge
you speak Oxford
you boast Harvard
in rhetoric
the people you say
are so happy
while starvation and drought plague the whole country
and you talk about yourself
and your big mansions
but what have you done
for the people you were asked
you skipped that question
with your favourite mask
went on about yourself
no question could be asked

you hypocrite!
you hypocrite!
puppet of the west
selling your people
to look your best
tell me!
tell me!
tell me right now
why you borrow everything
when the people can sow?
and why the population
must live to bow?!

PUT I IN THE MOOD

Put I in the mood
put I in the mood
tell I about where I come from
Africa
Slavery
Forefathers
Mothers
the Black Struggle
Liberation of flesh
and soul
put I in the mood
put I in the mood
in the
reggae jazz funk blues calypso
black music mood
in the good news
gospel redemption mood
in the Black Books Black Literature
cultural mood
in the pride for race
people
creation
salvation mood
in the joy and gladness mood
in the gospel freedom mood
put I in the mood
put I in the mood
and let I
let I feel irie
let I feel strong
and let I contribute
pay Tribute
Black Liberation!

SONG: CHANT!

mi hear this chant in many a song
mi hear this chant in generations
fire ago bun!
> down babylon
fire ago bun!
> down babylon
for they kingle a fire in dem captive space
brave warriors
ashanti!
congo-man
the marroon tribe
with nanny and cudjoe and great sam sharpe
paul bougle and william gordon
fire ago bun!
> down babylon
fire ago bun!
> down babylon
they kingle the torch of hope and faith
garvey and manley and bustamante
for the other generation to build upon
and to chant the old chant strong strong strong
fire ago bun!!
> down babylon
fire ago bun!!
> down babylon
and de fire did bun under oppression
and de fire did bun under suppression
civil rights leaders
freedom fighters
in the west and the south
it's liberation! liberation!
fire ago bun!!!
> down babylon
fire ago bun!!!
> down babylon.

ELECTION

(i)
e
  lec
    tion
e
  lec
    tion
gen er ral
e
  lec
    tion
e
  lec
    tion
corruption
division
fist sign
V sign
promises
promises
promises
promises.
  (ii)
a poverty
an class warfare
a de outcome
a de promises
our leaders rule
over us with a dividing whip
and use their devilish politics
to set brothers apart
brothers against brothers
bout Democracy better than Socialism
bout Socialism better than Democracy

(ii)
they serve us poisonous words for food
and confuse our minds with dem damn
politics politics
like force-ripe bananas
they prostitute themselves
as wholesome
and like stale bread
dey full a fungus
and maggots
stealing our votes
with bags of flour
and saltfish
chicken-back
and mackerel.

(iv)
a thousand a people
a die ina dem rigged
election system
you noh!
a heapa people ago tun
orphans an mourners
you noh!
a heapa people must
beg
and starve
walk naked
tun fool
and wuklis
you noh!
seaka dem dutty
bald heads
we call leaders and politicians.

(v)
words of war
war of words
words of bullets
bullets o words
is de state of confusion/corrruption
we reach
in our litte island
for de politician
give us evrything back and front
twisted and stuff with lies
like dem school days
fairy tales stories we tek fa G.C.E.

(vi)
so when we ago
sort out we
root out we
set straight we
life ina Jamaica
a when we ago
kill de
murder de
execute de
topple de
senseless violence
dat a mash-up we country
dat a mash-up we people?

(vii)
yes mi Idren
politician a preach/prosperity
how we economy
a pick up
how people a get more food
ya man!
a dem ting deh
a come over de radio
a dem ting deh
dem a print in de papers
a dem ting deh
dem a show on T.V./prosperity
it mussa mean drought an starvation
for a who de politician a fool
must be himself
an himself frienddem
dem an dem tourism
image making
 international scaffolding
and witholding of de truth
you noh!
for it can't be we
no spar! it can't be we
de polititian is mix up
in him isms
and prisms of words
idealogy of psyche
ideology of term
ideology of rhetoric
mad-ology
tinking dat him political
ideology of lies
can blind de whole nation
from the wickedness of de reality
dat him create an perpertrate/perpetually
like plagues on we.

SEAKA DEM POLITICS

we on so-so food
we on so-so food
belly haffe full wid so-so food
malnutrition plague
on so-so food
we haffe survive on so-so food
bush herb cure bellyache
bush herb haffe remedy sicknesses
we haffe survive on so-so food
if saltfish is at hand
we haffe flombodick it
if chicken-back is at hand
we ahffe flombodick it
we meat veg haffe stretch
like plantations of rice
we haffe drink beveridge water
an sing
we haffe eat we so-so food
an sing
ya man!
dey sey you must
belch an sing
give praise an sing
give thanks and sing
wid de family dem sing
wid de friend dem sing
singing soothes the soul
sweet words can taste like food
in de proper state of mind
wha no poison fatten
an wha a fatten must preserve us
tru deeze hard days
of political malfunction
hard days
of political witchcraft.

ISLAND

Why when I think of you
I cry
you
land of wood
and water
of sunshine
beauty and
nature
I was brought up
in you
schooled and
moulded in you
you gave me your
language
history
roots
but why when I
think of you
I cry
I see in you
while thinking deep
poverty
hardships
people
my people
in a hopeless condition
the young ones
turning to drugs
and corruption
the old ones
suffering suffering
from arthritis and bronchitis
with pains here pains there
weak tired overworked

I see the people
my people
driven to hillsides
mountains
to subservient farming
their children living on animal diet
stopping where they were born
hungry
why do I cry
when I think of you
you land
country
a tourist paradise
and my people's hell.

SEASON

The Season is come
winter season
COME TO JAMDOWN
NEGRIL
Tourism!
a cold northerly breeze
blow coldly from the sea
moisture laden Northers
it's a wind that can sting
bite
but the mouth of its anger
is subdued by the hot
sun
shine
hot
red hot
from dawn of day
to sunset
long sunny days
long sunny evenings.

WALKING THE BEACH

Under hot sunshine
in a jamdown land
under scorching sun
with an empty hand
I sit down and I walk
and I beg sometimes
desperately searching
to earn some dimes
I walk beaches
selling 'nice T-shirts'
walk beaches 'till
me foot dem hurt
walk beaches sometimes
paying to jah
walk beaches selling
sweet ganja.

BIG DREAD

Walking the beach
selling the sweet ganja
hoping to find
a rich buyer
I walk like a stranger
with a twisting head
saw big dread
the pol-
ice-
man
informer by trade
but he no look like one
hello big dread
what a lovely day
him looked at me
he had nothing to say
but he noticed me
from head to toe
trying to see if ganja
was on show
but I stuff my herb
in front of me brief
where only I and I is allowed to reach
he thought that I was clean
herbal free
so he went away
sit under a tree
where he watch everyday for a herb dealer
where he got his pay as an informer
news reached me that them shot him next day
collecting from babylon
his weekly pay.

BLACKER

The beach was swamped
with Rusty Babylon
searching everyone
which was only blackman
as-
king
ques-
ti-
on
about
the dead
'did you or didn't you
know big dread?'
at that time I was busy serving
a speckled face boy
who wasn't buying
how he come from England
don't mess with dope
except his interest
in peruvian coke
so I lectured the boy
about the real sensi
how a spliff or two
could get him irie
he agreed to have a draw
when the cops come along
with big black boots
in mi belly kick bang!
searching us mean
just to find we were clean
so they draped me white friend
and march
him
away
swear
they would beat me
'till me skin turn grey.

They chuck us in a cell
which was more like hell
as the darkness inside
was utter darkness
there were three spy holes
for oxygen
mosquitos
flies
and other devilment
the smell inside
un-
bear-
able-
made me shout
un-
con-
trol-
able-
it's a kennel
it's a kennel
it's a dog house
pit
the whole place
splattered
with human shit
my speckled face friend
start to bawl out his eye
'don't believe it,' he said
'it's all a big lie'
'calm yourself down'
a voice said from the dark
in
three years now
and I never mek a bark
jus sup it
jus sup it
from these evil shark
I was shook with fright

so I start feeling
I touch on a brada
who was down
kneeling
'blacker is the name
Ronny is the same
can't get up
mi whole body is lame
they beat me last night
they beat me everyday
'cause mi saw the big cop
when he rape a sister
fay
so he run me down the beach
and lock me up
plant the crime on me
and warn 'shut up'
sey dey wicked
dey wicked
dey in-
hu-
man
wicked
wicked
wicked
to tell the truth man'
he stop and start to cry
saying why
why
why
his own black brada
wishing him to die
'at evening time
they wet up the cell
a thing they do
they all take spell
so the mosquito
bite me to death

so I scared out mi life
die from fret
to let mi slide and slide
on thisslant boardbed
in misery
in misery
can't rest my head'
like a bomb explode
the door open
with four armed men
staring in the den
we all stand attention
without a mention
'till they order us out
to the big cop Stout
who freed the two of us
except blacker
who they kept in a cell
to batter
batter
'that no right officer
that no right at all'
blacker shouted out
when he got a fall
'mi no guilty fe nothing
in three years now
let me go
let me go'
then the gun went pow!!!

another one
another time
another black
brada kills his
own brada
wooooooooooo!
wooooooooooo!
a state of emergency
a state of emergency
but the doctors were too late
the spirit of the man couldn't wait
blacker was dead dead dead by then
in a state of authority
a state of hypocricy
the Babylon got off
free
in a state of bureaucracy
in a state of false judiciary
accidental death was the verdict.

I. TOURISM

The tourists tourists
crowded the beach
in dem nakedness
and different speech
you had the
pale white
real white
well suntanned
enjoying themselves
in a jamdown land
the beautiful hotels
in their moderness
are of stark contrast
to the wilderness
where many of the people
live in bitterness
in their board house
tatch house
and ramshack
under big broad tree
or a comfy grass patch
they eat what they sow
and they starve sometimes
lamenting on the scale
of the system's crimes.

MR RASS CLARK

They don't want us on the beach
'cause we 'black like tar'
they want us in the bushes
quite far far far
but me have a black friend called Mr Rass
him no tek insult
him fass fass fass

him fishing at nights
on the lovely beach
where the best sea fish
is at an easy reach

he park his kart
on the hotel bound'
and as it reach midday
the tourist surround
'hot fish with pepper
selling quick so rush'
the tourist buy
with them eager lust
eating up the fish
which to them look 'new'
licking them fingers
when the pepper bun 'koo'

a red face boy
said him own the beach
as him big hotel
stretch where the water reach
him clear him throat
and called Rass aside
telling him rules
by which to abide

how 'the tourist hate
the bad language'
how his fish is cheap
his bread sandwich
Rass trade good
he no get fardon
thinking that Rass would
beg pardon
but Rass tell the boy
he go touch him kart
or even to move it
from where it park
him turn bright red
start to mumble words
which sound loud to Rass
as few could be heard
he point his finger
in Rass 'black face'
calling dutty names
that hurt
disgrace
so Rass throw a handful
a sand in his face
punch him and kick him
without any grace
a stucky little American
intervened
receiving a fist
that left him lean

Rass left them both
in the sand
in pain
to serve his customers
on His! Domain!

II. TOURISM

Guarded beach
and guided tour
around the sea coast
and back by four
when the scene is set
for the lovely sunset
where the drinks
start to shower
for the happy hour
the ganja start to
burn for the late party
where the sick and disease
looks very hearty
where the false dreadlocks
prostituted themselves
where the young black girls
start to sell themselves
where the rich start to pass
their rich disease
their
her-
pes
sy-
phil-
is
gon-
or-
rhea
where fatal drugs
are in exchange
where the nice and good
must get change
where the whoredom
start in hotel room
where many black lives
are sure to spell doom.

DARKNESS! NIGHT!

Darkness! Night!
the Northers blew by my right ear
with a wheezing sound
with a tingling feeling
Darkness! Night!
I pull my sweatsuit top
over my orange colour T-shirt
my 'nice T-shirt'
hands in pockets
and walked up the beach
Darkness! Night!
my feet got wet
sea water splash
to sand bank level
and in the darkness
the howling of the sea
dead spirits howling
bawling
'Darkness! Night!'
I took out a spliff
from my cigarette box
light it up
puff pull swallow
puff pull swallow
repeatedly
until the beach caught fire
'Babylon end!'
I controlled myself
saw waves rising
people screaming drowning
puff pull swallow
puff pull swallow
I left my body
I was

I was
I didn't know-where
but days
flashes of recent days
came back to me
but I was
I was
nowhere
'Babylon Judge!'
I controlled myself
wondering if I was
in the sea
or on the sand
or somewhere safe
I knew I was moving
so consciously I closed my eyes
shook my head from side to side
opened my eyes
saw lightenings
thunderings
heard dogs barked
felt asphalt under my feet
my barefeet

'till one car went by
two three four five six seven eight nine . . . .
puff pull swallow
puff pull swallow
'nowhere to hide
to go
Babylon fall!'
three spirits leapt out of me
the first went across the road
the second followed
the third went across
looked left
looked right
I followed

safely
cross the road
Darkness! Night!
I consciously walked
along the pavement
until I reached
SOON COME
it was jammed
bodies swaying
to reggae
calypso
funk soul
to music
music
music
I saw Jah Mickey Mouse
who I gave the remainder
of my spliff
my Sensi
My Sensimelia Superior Red
my brain in pain
heavy
my head a large stone
heavy
my optic nerves
falsifying my vision
showing me wrong images
for Jah Mickey Mouse
flew through the window
and bounced back
then he flew across the dance floor
and I laughed
I heard him shouted
'mystic! wicked Sensi!
Iya ites!'
he was laughing
I was laughing

Darkness! Night!
brada Mickey Mouse and I chant
through the darkness night
well red!
well dread!
well irie!
'blood and fire!!!!!!'

me an papa mickey
in darkness
can't see
Gan-
Ja
cloud we eyes
an we brains not
free
our mind and brain
are on a spree
so we talk and we laugh
and we shout sometimes
we go for days
without a bite
we go crazy
an we laugh too much
we sit an we shirk
work is a rush
un-
con-
scious-
ly
we whore all night
things we shouldn't do
look blasted right
an we smoke Gan-
Ja
'It's out of sight!'
we smoke Gan-
Ja
from dusk till light
now I think back in time
much clearer
an able
to say

IT SWEETER OUT YA!
free from the influence
of nature's herb
my mind at peace
it's not dis-
turb
for my head
my head
is a Gan-
Ja
free zone
my head
my head
is a Gan-
Ja
free zone.

A YOUNG COUPLE

LOVE AT FIRST SIGHT

Your love I cried
is wonderfully sweet
I knew you were mine
from the first we meet
your face was set
with a welcoming smile
the way you dressed
was a special style
your body looked great
in your see-through dress
I gasped from love
I was so helpless
darling you are mine
I said in my heart
I bought you a drink
there we start
the club was jammed
with many other girls
they were silver
you were the pearls
we danced for a while
then we start to caress
we kissed there touched here
lost in the bliss
after that night
we made our plan
love at first sight
we were man and woman.

PROBLEMS

I lost my job in
the world recession
the car and the house
became a broken plan
we lived instead in
our council flat
a one room shack
that was far from hot
it was cold and damped
and breeds insects
the walls were bare
with holed defects
a misery you might say
if you hear about it
for three long years
it was stinking shit
it affected our marriage
in many many ways
frustration and depression
attacked many days.

HER POINT OF VIEW

I know you are the man
and I respect that
but you can't sit around
expect to be fat
for I have a mind
and I have a soul
you are not the only one
we are both in the hole
if you don't get a job
then we have to split
not going to live
in this kind of pit
for its been three years now
it can't prolong
you your promises
should both be hung.

WORRIED ABOUT ME

I understand your feelings
tears are in your eyes
pressures plague your consciousness
you see me as a poor man
with confused ideas struggling
lost hopes immature
fearful for the burdens life brings
you are worried about me
my thoughts aren't actions
my promises are unfulfilled
but I
my consciousness sheds doubts
I am weary of repeated thoughts
I meditate upon time's fleeting time
seeing my future within the day
a job through my mind's eye
all fading from reality
ideas are cultivated daily in my head
forming a world with a way out
my heart beats with hope
courage upholds my strength
dismissing the fear to search
the darkness
the darkness
to find.

THE BIG BIG WORLD

For I am waiting on their handouts
being forced into crime
when there must be another way
to eat without a dime
for there is the world
the big big world
there is the world
the big big world
it's defeat if I beg
to thief is folly
but I must find something
to feed our belly
for there is the world
the big big world
there is the world
the big big world
I'll seek and find
ask and get
knock 'till open
wait won't fret
for there is the world
the big big world
there is the world
the big big world.

JOB HUNTING

I went out to search
but I didn't succeed
the last interview
was just a false lead
I felt so hurt
that I couldn't impress
they wanted a girl
in sexy dress
they were looking
for grades and a pretty Juliet
o'levels a'levels
college graduate
but I'll be going
to search tomorrow again
hoping to find some
joy not pain
in the meantime dear
let us conserve
watch how you spend
we have to preserve
'your talk is sick!
you are so helpless
you are a boy! not a man
you make me depress'
I am sorry
for appealing
to you that way
I didn't make myself
so.............
so I have to stay
can't you see that time is rough
why are you trying to make things tough
told you many times
that we have to have hope
am not like the others
won't hang by a rope

we just have to live
on what we've got
thank God bless God
food in the pot
I tell you
thank God bless God
food in the pot.

QUARREL

I told you the truth
but you cursed me tonight
you should be carefull I said
our money is tight
our pittance must stretch
from days to week
must spend it proper
for safely keep
you can't buy this
and you can't buy that
the bare essentials
you should have got
you refused to listen
to what I said
as if you rather hungry-belly
and a big-fat-head
'I am a woman of the world
and I have my ways
a blasted ten pounds
can't serve for three days'
I take your point
but you didn't buy meat
with tin this
and box that
ends can't meet.

SEPARATE

Oh the pangs!
the pangs of a love
that I thought was real
was only the folly
of my high ideals
rings on our fingers
in a married life
you by my side
my dear little wife
'our love so sweet
that we can't separate'
that's what we say
in hope and faith
but we quarreled everyday
over simple things
the love that we had
had taken wings
and now the blues
the blues of a love
that was so untrue
has opened my eyes
to a different view
something new
now not you
for love should be real
and not at first sight
a learning to love
instead of fights!

REFLECTION

Man can change
and so his plan
I am a bachelor again
without a woman
I see you many times
in countless dreams
always the girl
with eyes that gleam
but loving your body
was hard to sustain
at times I got bored
other times I felt strained
for love can't grow
on carnal lust
which exist today
and tomorrow turn dust
it grows from the heart
and it needs nourishing
not as obligation
but natural loving!